A strikingly original debut and a celebration of the remarkable, everyday process of making and remaking: of story, of clothing, and of ourselves.

In *Patchwork*, a charming and evocative sewist's diary, Maddie Ballard explores the making (and sometimes remaking) of seventeen specific garments over a period of great change in her life—from a jacket lined with the embroidered Cantonese names of her female ancestors, to a dressing gown made as a gift for a dear friend, to an eco-friendly, zero-waste dress.

As the wardrobe grows, so too does Maddie's journey. From her first off-kilter dresses and coats to perfectly fitting pants, readers follow along as she learns to navigate the world around her and how she sees herself in it—both as she is and as she hopes to be. Stitch by stitch, word by word, Maddie drafts her own patterns for ways of living. Throughout the diary, delightful illustrations bring Maddie's creations to life on the page.

With a focus on the practical comfort and pleasure provided by sewing in a time of personal renewal, *Patchwork: A Sewist's Diary* is lyrical, soothing, and wise—a warmhearted celebration of the value of craft in the mod

"A beautifully observed meditation on the emotional resonance of clothing and sewing. It will make you look with a new eye on what you wear and how it was made."
—**Tracy Chevalier**,
New York Times bestselling author of *The Glassmaker*

"Maddie Ballard makes making clothes into a celebration of living and suffering and finding joy. Wonderful."
—**Victoria Finlay**,
author of *Fabric: The Hidden History of the Material World*

"Nimble, surprising, edifying, and even sexy, Maddie Ballard's *Patchwork* is a document of living and being lived in, a record of staying enlivened through catastrophe, and a graceful experiment in imagining how the tactile world might be the real one."
—**Emma Copley Eisenberg**,
bestselling author of *Housemates*

"A beautifully layered narrative that celebrates how the simple act of sewing our own clothing can help us define ourselves and find belonging. Maddie's writing is a joy to read."
—**Clara Parkes**,
author of *Vanishing Fleece: Adventures in American Wool*

"A gorgeous, tender exploration of the craft of sewing and how we carve out spaces for ourselves."
—**Nina Mingya Powles**,
author of *Small Bodies of Water*

"Maddie Ballard's *Patchwork* deftly and poetically reminds us that sewing is more than an act of creation. It reminds us that a sewing is an act of self-creation too."
— **Betsy Greer**,
author of *Knitting for Good!*

"Maddie Ballard's *Patchwork*, with its beautifully woven reflections, is evidence of how making things with our hands can change us—and the world."
—**Nina Montenegro**,
author of *Mending Life*

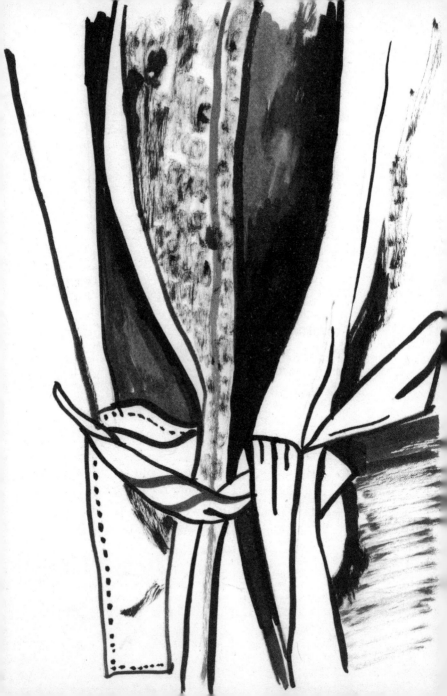

PATCH WORK

a sewist's diary

MADDIE BALLARD

Illustrated by Emma Dai'an Wright

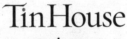

A zando IMPRINT

NEW YORK

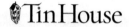

This is a work of nonfiction, except for a handful of names and identifying details changed to respect individuals' privacy.

Text copyright © 2024 by Maddie Ballard
Interior illustrations copyright © 2024 by Emma Dai'an Wright

First US Edition 2025
Previously published as *Bound: A Memoir of Making and Remaking* in 2024 in the UK by The Emma Press Ltd.

Zando supports the right to free expression and the value of copyright. The purpose of copyright is to encourage writers and artists to produce the creative works that enrich our culture. Thank you for buying an authorized edition of this book and for comply- ing with copyright laws by not reproducing, scanning, uploading, or distributing this book or any part of it without permission. If you would like permission to use material from the book (other than for brief quotations embodied in reviews), please contact connect@zandoprojects.com.

Tin House is an imprint of Zando.
zandoprojects.com

Manufacturing by Versa Press
Cover and text design by Beth Steidle

The publisher does not have control over and is not responsible for author or other third-party websites (or their content).

978-1-963108-48-4 (hardcover)
978-1-963108-55-2 (ebook)

10 9 8 7 6 5 4 3 2 1

Manufactured in the United States of America

for 婆婆

Contents

First Love	3
Work	9
Moral Fibre	15
Second Skin	23
Hard	31
Soft	39
Silver Lining	47
Ease	55
Cut One Pair	61
Undoing	67
Bound	73
Use	81
Cut One Self	89
Common Thread	97
Care Instructions	107
Patchwork	113
Edge	121
Notes	127
Acknowledgements	129

Patchwork

THE ROOM SMELLS OF DUST AND WASHED COTton. In my lap, a pile of cloth; at my feet, a patch of snipped threads. The scissors rasp at a flex of my wrist, a single-syllable incantation.

Again and again I fumble with needle and thread. This is a love story.

First Love

*Dove grey linen-cotton,
dove grey polyester thread //
Anna Allen Demeter Dress*

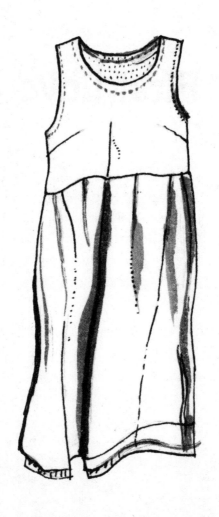

WINTER. NEW PLYMOUTH. WE HAVE SWAPPED London's pea green parks and sooty pubs for the black beaches and salt of the West Coast. We are sort of home but not exactly, because home vanished some time ago, perhaps when we were leaving stricken England, our lives rushed into two suitcases, wearing gloves and N95s.

In our room in your parents' house, we wake to the sound of tūī in the kōwhai. We walk the dog and go swimming—sometimes in the icy sea, sometimes at the big public pool, where the fearless ten-year-olds on school holidays vault into deep water without ever looking down. You take me to the top of Paritutu, where the sea stretches out and out like a vast dreaming unconscious. Each morning, the snow-tipped peak of Mount Taranaki catches the eye, a compass of meaning I can't read. Your parents pour us each two-glass-sized glasses of wine, roast chickens for dinner, lend us wetsuits and trail maps.

I love your parents. I love you. Your face is nearest to me of anyone's in the world, and every day I'm overwhelmed by your beauty: your pianist's hands, your patience, the deep safe scent of you. We are anxious, in limbo, but we don't fight. We have never known our story better.

While you work the freelance hours you've cobbled together, I write cover letters I get no response to and scroll Instagram. One day an acquaintance posts a photo of a skirt she's made in cobalt linen. The fabric is so beautiful it looks sentient. The word that comes to mind is *Maybe*. Your mum has an old sewing machine that belonged to her mum, which she unboxes for the first time in years, along with her sewing kit. This is my first introduction to all the notions—the official collective noun—involved in sewing: boxes of rusted thimbles, loose hooks and eyes, spools of thread in every colour, scissors large and small. There are names to learn, buttons to sort: a grounding, material world.

Your mum shows me how to wind the bobbin, go fishing for the bobbin thread with the needle, press down just hard enough to start the seam. When I make a mistake, she says, *Don't worry* and finds an unpicker in the box of spare needles. Her machine has no backstitch function, so every seam must be begun then lifted, turned and gone back over. I learn to be slow. I strain. The hours turn gentle.

Once I can sew a straight stitch, I decide my first project will be the Anna Allen Demeter Dress, which is marked 'beginner'. I choose a dove grey linen-cotton blend from the local opshop and print the pattern on your mum's printer. It takes me a whole day to tape together and cut out, but I have a whole day to spare. The day I start, you are sitting on the couch behind me, writing advertising copy. For the first time in a while, we are both busy.

My first darts. My first shoulder seam. Over and over, I follow instructions I don't understand, certain I'm doing something wrong, and over and over, the fabric responds. I stay-stitch the neckline and armholes, then attach strange, diagonal strips of fabric around the curve on what seems like the wrong side. Everything frays. But after turning, tucking, pressing, and stitching, it becomes a recognisable if slightly untidy bodice and I feel like God. I tell the dog; I tell you. I am so thrilled, I tell everybody. I go on to the skirt, pressing each seam impatiently with your mum's ancient iron. I fuss, I coax. I ask of the linen a metamorphosis, from flat sheaf to three-dimensional case for the body and, mostly, it obeys. I can't imagine it becoming less miraculous.

It takes me two whole days, sewing right until bedtime, to finish the dress. I've made and unpicked so many mistakes that the carpet is furred with discarded thread. The dress, which resembles a Victorian nightgown, is a bit too big, with crooked, flimsy pockets and a poorly topstitched waist. Even after reading the instructions three times, I couldn't figure out the gathering, so the skirt has a bunch of uneven pleats instead. But I love it—as much for the care it has prised from me as for its shape on my body. I can't believe how long the sewing process has taken. *This is the level of labour that goes into every $10 dress on the H&M sale rack!* I tell you, in astonishment. It is a privilege not to have to—not to be able to—rush.

When I put it on to show you, you laugh, kindly, at my face as much as the dress. But I don't care that you think I look ridiculous. I sew every day until I can do something different.

Work

*Pale pink dachshund-
patterned cotton canvas,
pale pink polyester thread //
Tessuti Apron*

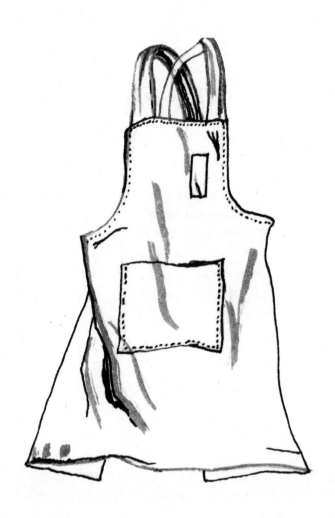

WHEN WE MOVE TO AUCKLAND, MY GRANDMA offers me her sewing machine, a hardy Pfaff. I can recall her hemming the family's trousers on this machine throughout my childhood—the chugging noise held steady by her foot in its sequinned slipper. She says she can't see the stitches anymore, so she'd like me to have it.

When I go to pick it up, 婆婆 | Por Por presses on me not just the Pfaff, but also a box of tangled thread spools, a container of pins, and a basket of orphaned buttons. Some of these belonged to my great-grandmothers. I was frightened of their harsh faces, the unhesitating way they hit me across the hands when I misbehaved. It was not until I was older that I could imagine why they had the faces they did; that their lives had involved, in intricate and terrible ways, more suffering than anyone I knew. They did not sew as a hobby, could not have conceived of being a *sewist*, that gender-neutral, leisure-connoting term in use today. As always when I think of them, my life seems heavy with luck. I accept all their sewing paraphernalia.

The sewing machine and notions follow us all around the city. We house-sit and care for lots of other people's animals; we sleep on an air mattress at my parents'; we keep half our clothes in our car. We move to an inner-city apartment that's being rented to us for much less than it's worth, on the condition that we might have to leave at short notice. We do. We end up flatting with two strangers. Later we will realise that we have moved—shoes, notebooks, cake tins, thread spools—sixteen times in the space of a year. You work full-time but remotely, isolated from the rest of your London-based team. I work three days a week at the library, social but ill-paid. Neither of us is quite happy, but we walk around the waterfront each evening and love every detail worth loving, and I have lots of time to sew, which is a way of escaping reality.

I lower the needle and the world recedes. The process of sewing a garment—printing the pattern, tracing and cutting, sewing the first and the second and the fiftieth seam—is a lesson in taking your time. There is a language of touch to be learned, too—the crunkle of freshly washed denim in the hand; the unexpected weight of silk velvet. I spend a whole afternoon wondering if the words *tactile* and *textile* might be related. They're not, but *text* and *textile* are: both works of weaving. I learn, over the course of many sewing sessions, that French seams are my favourite way to finish fabric and that my legs are shorter than I think. I learn to sew buttonholes and flip out a shirt using something called the 'burrito method'. I acquire more discrete, tangible skills than in several years. I stop buying clothes.

Nine months pass in this way. Then, somehow, I land a journalism job. I become the deputy editor of a food magazine, writing and sub-editing stories. Here there are other things to learn: the one-two punch of writing a header and sell, how to get a quote out of a taciturn chef, what *pet nat* stands for. Our magazine is beautiful, known for its luminous close-ups of the light on a plate of tomatoes or the blush on a platter of lamb. Every day verges on unbearably busy, but I thrill to the deadline, the close-up focus and bright speed of it. When I tell somebody where I work, they say *Oh I love that magazine!* and everything shines.

The pace of my sewing slows. Mostly, I make midi-length work dresses, taking a week over each one. But after two cooking-heavy months at the magazine, I realise I need a new apron: my old one is starred with sauce splatters no stain remover will lift.

For the fabric, I choose a pale pink canvas covered with navy blue line drawings of sausage dogs. It's silly and perfect. I cut a Tessuti Apron and sew it up in a single afternoon. I choose this pattern for its practicality—the big front pocket, the pull-on design and crossed back straps—but I tinker, too. The curved edges are all finished with homemade bias tape, rather than just messily folded up, and I add a small breast pocket for a teaspoon. I raise the neckline slightly, for extra coverage, and attach the facing differently from how the pattern instructs. By this point, I have practised enough to know how to make these tweaks. The work of learning is a whole year deep.

I slip it over my head and make us good things to eat. There are coconut-heady dals; focaccia pooled with grassy olive oil and sea salt; green tea rice and salmon; peach tart. We eat together each night and no pasta sauce ever gets on my clothes. Between sewing, writing, and cooking, my life is full of making. In every act, I savour.

Moral Fibre

*Black and beige gingham
linen, tan polyester thread //
Self-drafted zero-waste dress*

WHEN AUCKLAND IS DARK WITH RAIN, I DECIDE to make a winter work dress using some long-hoarded black and beige gingham linen. The fabric is so heavy and fine, I can't bear for a scrap to go to waste—so I decide on a zero-waste dress.

'Zero-waste' sewing means sewing with nothing left behind, or maybe just a shred for your scraps box. Every last piece made useful and precious. Because they must be cut entirely of tessellating shapes, most zero-waste patterns rely on rectangles, which lend themselves to loose shapeliness rather than form-fitting garments. But the alchemy of sewing is never more pronounced than when you're working only with rectangles: the feat by which flat pieces of fabric are turned, by snip and stitch, into something that can hold a person.

I've been thinking a lot about zero-waste sewing lately. Thanks to my new job, I can afford to buy fabric for many more dresses, but I'm wary of starting to live less lightly.

When I look into it, I find that textile production and wastage are worse for the planet than I imagined. Annual greenhouse gas emissions from textile production total more than international flights and maritime shipping combined. Clothing production doubled between 2000 and 2015, yet more than half of fast fashion is disposed of in less than a year. Globally, one garbage truck of textiles is landfilled or incinerated every second. Not to mention that garment and textile workers—75 million people worldwide, mostly in the Global South, mostly women—often work ten to sixteen-hour days in appalling conditions for poverty-level wages.

Sewing gives you greater control over your fashion consumption and can be a more affordable route to sustainable fashion than buying solely from pricey ethical brands. But sewing sustainably—like shopping sustainably—involves asking hard questions. Where, how, and by whom was the fibre grown or produced? Who dyed and finished the textile, and did the process compromise their health? How did the fabric get to me? How many times will I wear the garment I'm making? What will I do with it if I stop wanting to wear it, or if it becomes irreparably damaged? Answering these questions takes work, and sometimes, like everyone, I'm lazy.

There are sewists who buy only natural fibres, to avoid microplastic-shedding synthetics; who eschew cotton, which is water-intensive to produce; who buy only fabric they're going to use straightaway, so as not to hoard and overconsume; who opt solely for second-hand or dead stock fabrics, which would otherwise be landfilled. There are sewists who sew only a handful of garments each year, building clever capsule wardrobes. There are sewists who get into natural dyeing; sewists who give up printed patterns in favour of electronic projections to save paper; sewists who save all their scraps for quilts or cushion stuffing; sewists who glamorise mending. I admire these efforts and think each one helps, but I know I could never commit to them all. I love thrifting a length of mystery fabric with no immediate plans. I love sewing with cotton, although whenever possible, I buy organic or dead stock. I don't want a capsule wardrobe, because some days I want to wear a Barbie pink jumpsuit and others I crave the quiet of black. I don't think it's morally reprehensible to want a wardrobe that contains both. Making my own clothes already slows and focuses my consumption—and I sew for pleasure just as much as to opt out of fast fashion.

I make my zero-waste dress to last. I lay out the full three metres of gingham linen and plot a cutting plan for maximum floofiness, stretching my high school maths. Two rectangles for the bodice, two larger ones for the skirt. Two generous rectangles for romantic gathered sleeves, then long skinny rectangles to make the sleeve cuff channels, ties, and a sash. Four big squares for pockets. I use the full expanse of fabric and there are only two off-cuts: the semicircles snipped to form the front and back necklines.

Linen is one of the more sustainable fabrics available, but I can't claim to know exactly where the flax for this linen was grown and woven, whether anyone imperilled their health during its processing, and how exactly the textile reached me. I feel guilty about this, especially when I realise these are questions I should have asked earlier, when I was buying the fabric. But the opposite of a thoughtless consumer is not a saint: it's a conscious consumer. I don't think you need to sew only zero-waste garments out of thrifted hemp to make a difference. Instead, I think it's about sewing intentionally, with purpose and care, and being mindful within your means. The most environmentally friendly clothes are the ones you wear and wear—and in this case, the best thing I can do is use up what I have and make my dress to last.

Sewing this dress is slow; an ache of care. I bias bind the neckline on the inside with scraps of the dove grey linen-cotton from my first Demeter Dress, and take my time topstitching the curves. When gathering the waist and the tops of the sleeves, I bother to run two lines of basting stitches to achieve the most even gathers. The whole garment is French-seamed, for a finish that will last. It takes three weeks to complete, longer than I have spent on a dress in several months, and I notice my body responding. My neck gets stiff from bending over my machine. My legs, after hours of sitting, grow numb. I think of the women sitting in hot rooms in Shenzhen and Dhaka, sewing the next season's $20 jeans for a pittance. Their bodies must protest too. I think about the fact that I came to this labour by choice, that I'm sewing for myself in a bedroom in an affluent suburb of Auckland, using fabric I could easily afford. I think about the fact that I used to buy those $20 jeans and that there was a time when I couldn't afford anything else. It's all so complicated and

everybody is complicit. I can't solve any of it. But I can try to make with care.

When the dress is finally finished, the cuffs are a little wonky and, in keeping with using every last bit of fabric, not all the seams are pattern-matched. But I know I will wear it until it can't be worn anymore, until the fibres, rubbed down with age, literally begin to disappear. If I unpick my hardy polyester thread it can even be composted, once it's too old for the pieces to be reused. It satisfies something in me, imagining its disintegration—the sturdy flax fibres, made textile, then garment, becoming soil once more.

Second Skin

Black six-wale cotton corduroy,
black polyester thread, pale pink linen,
scarlet cotton embroidery thread,
25 mm black corozo buttons //
Fabrics-Store.com Paola Workwear Jacket

IT'S THE LAST WEEK IN JANUARY WHEN MY COLleague sends the team an email to review. It's meant for our many subscribers and opens chattily by wondering whether it's correct to say 'Chinese New Year' or 'Lunar New Year'. *I did some digging and you know what, I have no idea who's right*, my colleague writes. *This year at least, it seems like both the Chinese and Lunar New Years fall on the same day, so how about we split the difference and just refer to it as the Year of the Tiger? Sounds cooler anyway.* My whole body feels hot and numb as I read these sentences, which seem to be saying *These differences don't really matter, right? I don't know, and you don't know, and so: who cares.*

I wonder how to respond. Two other colleagues come back with praise for the funniness of other parts of the email. Nobody says anything about the first paragraph. I write a very careful reply, recommending 'Lunar New Year' because many cultures celebrate the beginning of the lunar calendar—correcting without scolding.

I think, as I always do at such moments, of more aggressive encounters I've had: the man who shouted a slur from his car, the guest who asked if I was the help, the two men pulling their eyes at me outside the train station. This is mild by contrast, but I think its mildness makes it more insidious. I wonder how my email reads to everybody else. My colleague makes the change with good grace, although nobody apologises.

Several hours later I still feel ill about it. To keep my helplessness at bay, I cut out an oversized black corduroy jacket—six-wale corduroy, soft enough to drowse in. I've been meaning to make this jacket for months. I made an identical one for your birthday and wear it so often, the sleeves rolled back three times, that you've started hanging it on my side of the closet.

Corduroy sulks. When I brush my hand across it, the fibres refuse to lie down smoothly in one direction. If I don't cut all the pattern pieces facing the same way, the garment will look patchy in the light. It's messy to sew with corduroy too, fluff freckling the carpet and catching in the bobbin case. But I'm using a favourite pattern, the Paola Workwear

Jacket, and I don't even need the instructions. I turn the flat-felled seams quickly and surely; I eyeball the pocket placement with ease. I sew seam after seam, seething and methodical, and I've rarely made something so free of mistakes.

I know, when I try on the jacket the next morning, that I will wear this all the time: it makes me look like myself. But it needs a lining. I want a jacket with a rich inner life. I wonder about embroidering a line from a favourite poem, but I'm still heavy and hurt from yesterday. I shrug off poetry like an unwanted hand on my shoulder.

Instead, I ring 婆婆 | Por Por, the most cheerful person I know. *Hi* 麗麗 | *Lai Lai!* she chirps down the phone at me, like always. *How are you, how is your work?* She says it exactly like this, *How is your work?*, and I think first not of my job at the magazine but of the jacket I'm working on, and this essay I'm writing. It turns out I know exactly what I want to embroider. I ask her to write down the characters of her name and my mother's name and her mother's

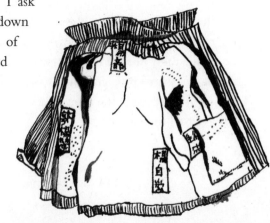

name and mine—all the female family members, as far back as she can remember. She's bemused by the request, but when I visit her that weekend she gives me the names, each on its own slip of paper: 麗瑶, 自愛, 錦雲, 文麗… Each of them contains other meanings, so the slips are starred, too, with *beauty* and *grace* and *love*. I trace each name with tailors' chalk onto scraps of palest shell pink linen. This will be my lining.

My anger dissipates. The Lunar New Year comes and goes, and we toss the 魚生 | yu sheng salad as high as the light fittings, and we eat the enormous prawns and the fatty, salty 烧肉 | siu yuk, and we exchange, as always, wishes for each other's prosperity. It takes me several sittings to embroider all the names on my linen in lucky red thread: the names of those who made new lives for themselves away from war, in a country where the new year happens resolutely on 1 January. When I'm done, I cut the names out and slip-stitch the pieces of linen into the jacket with black thread. There's no particular configuration: two are mostly hidden in the sleeves, while three dot the back. I sew in my name, a nudge bigger than a postage stamp, where a label might go. 婆婆's name is at the front, where I will always see it as I pull the jacket closed.

The evening I complete my jacket, I move yours back to your side of the closet. I wear mine at least once a week, the secret of the lining held close to my skin like a kind of external knowledge. I look braver than I feel.

Hard

*Taupe stretch cotton twill,
caramel cotton canvas, black cotton twill,
indigo selvedge denim, assorted polyester
thread, midweight fusible interfacing,
20 mm coconut buttons, 23 mm corozo
buttons, 18 cm YKK zips //
Peppermint Wide Leg Pants,
Merchant & Mills Eve Trousers*

DURING THE LONGEST LOCKDOWN, I FIND MYSELF sewing mainly trousers. Not the elastic-waisted kind, which would make sense for someone whose only interaction with the outside world is on Zoom, but the sort with flies and stiff waistbands: what are known, in the sewing community, as 'hard pants'.

Even the simplest hard pants pattern involves many fiddly pieces—fly, fly guard, pocket bags, belt loops—and a series of subtle curves whose shape cannot be fudged if you want them to sit right. You need not only fabric and thread, but also waistband interfacing, buttons, and perhaps also zips, snaps, or rivets. Trouser-weight fabric can be onerous for all but the sturdiest machines, and many seams must be stitched with painstaking slowness, often after hand-basting. Finally, they're notoriously difficult to fit, because hard pants have to embrace so many different parts of you: the knobbly dip at the small of your back; the bow and sweep of your buttocks, one often a little bigger than the other; the swell of your hips; the inlet of your waist; the shape—likely never before considered—of your pubis. Every body is different. Figuring out how to fit yours takes time and careful attention.

I'm not in the mood, during these weeks inside, to look closely at my body. We own a beautiful full-length mirror in a rimu frame, a gift for our life together from your parents. But I don't like my wobbly, pale body right now. My stomach spills over the waistband of a skirt that fit last year, and I will not meet my eyes in the mirror. I can't bear any extra discomfort. We spend more time than usual in bed, watching soothing films. We are always hungry, so I make us steamed buns, plush and gentle, and bowls of dumplings with chilli oil and black vinegar. Each of us is irritable, in need of care.

Still, I want the absorption of making hard pants, which means engaging with my body. One morning, I stand in front of the mirror in my underwear and take my measurements for the first time in six months. They are bigger than before and I feel a sting of guilt—but I can make a pair of trousers that fit my current body perfectly.

Before this lockdown I had made two pairs of hard pants using the Peppermint Wide Leg Pants pattern—an enthusiastic, wonky first pair in a tofu-coloured twill; and a second pair in caramel canvas that pinched in the crotch. The paper pattern in the size I've cut out is too small now, so I choose a new pattern, one that can be posted to me because we don't have a printer: the Eve Trousers by Merchant & Mills. I choose a light, crisp black cotton twill from my stash and scoop the front crotch curve slightly on the pattern piece, because I know now that's the amendment I usually have to make for pants patterns. I alter nothing else.

It sews up okay. The length is right and the lapped zip was a coup, but there's too much fabric around the back crotch curve and the straight waistband gapes. When I ask you for a second opinion, you are lying on the couch cradling your laptop and reply, barely glancing over, that they look good. But I suspect you have stopped being able to see things properly. I'm still going out every day for a walk, but you spend long stretches never

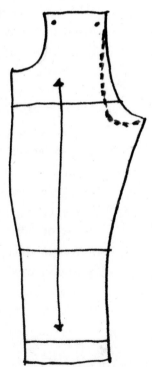

going outside. I make and make—cinnamon rolls, watercolour birthday cards, trousers for the unimaginable reopening of the world—but you don't feel like making anything. I grow more frustrated than is fair. We have hardly left the apartment in more than eight weeks and I've looked at everything in my life twice now.

I want to feel better. I want to feel good—and sewing, I think, is a way to make yourself feel good in your specific body. Like all microcosms, the sewing community is not immune to fatphobia, racism, ableism, and prejudices of all kinds. But there is so much body positivity in this space too. Several popular pattern companies, including TFS Patterns, Muna and Broad, Friday Pattern Company, and Closet Core Patterns, offer highly inclusive size ranges. Some pattern companies label their size ranges with letters (A, B, C) rather than traditional specifications (8, 10, 12 . . . or S, M, L)—a small but freeing detail. Sewing Instagram is populated with sewists of all sizes recording the fitting struggles they've had and noting their pattern adjustments. There are plenty of radiant fat sewists, celebrating their right to feel good in their bodies, in clothes that fit well. Whatever you want to sew, there's someone with a body like yours who has sewn something similar.

Beyond the community, there's the freedom of the act of sewing itself. Fabric is generous: you make the clothes to fit you, rather than the other way around. Every garment is bespoke by default, and your figure, not some 'ideal' figure, is the centre. Homemade trousers should hold your living and singular body with tenderness. You do not have to settle for something fitting *quite well*.

I read up on pants fitting adjustments and start the Eves again. My second pair, made from heavy, buttery denim, have a shallower back crotch curve, slimmed thighs, and a curved waistband. They fit so well I could cry. My stocky legs feel strong and shapely in these pants. My arse sits high and defined, framed by ideally placed pockets. My body is my only lasting home, I remember—I want, I need, to love it.

Soft

*Forest green merino, black merino, pale grey merino, assorted polyester thread //
Papercut Patterns Rise and Fall Turtleneck*

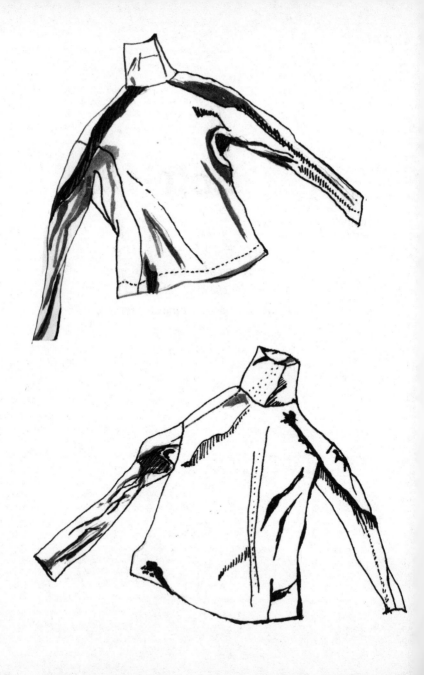

MOTHS COME THROUGH THE OPEN WINDOW AT night, mistaking our lamps for the moon. Our apartment is home to so many dim wings that it's easy not to notice them. I see the first of the wrong kind in November, by which point it is too late.

⤳

The common clothes moth, *Tineola bisselliella*, has existed since at least Roman times. All through the seasons of human suffering and striving, outliving empires and famines, this little hay-coloured moth has moved where people move. Its larvae eat natural fibres above all—cotton, linen, hemp, silk, wool—leaving fine holes in their wake.

Clothes moth devastation must have been far greater at a time when all cloth was solely the product of human

labour. But textiles remain precious, even when they are woven by machine: the crisp hand of cotton poplin, the vapour of silk georgette, the soft prickle of wool.

In the darkness of our closets, I set traps that grow furred with bodies.

I kill many.

It feels like the violence goes two ways, but it's an illusion. The moth larvae do not eat my clothes to spite me. They eat them to stay alive.

When I snap the flickering bodies out of the air, you roll your eyes. But when we find a tiny, wriggling larva on your favourite coat, you concede. We wash everything, pack the woollens into the freezer, and vacuum the gaps between every floorboard. We seal the windows in the summer heat and set off the bombs, waiting out the fumigation in Albert Park, where the beds are riotous with flowers whose mood we cannot match.

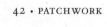

∽

They're beautiful, palest gold and iridescent. When I sweep up afterwards, their bodies everywhere are light and shining as wishes.

∽

Even after the fumigation, I can't relax. Fresh traps show that we haven't eradicated all the moths. You are exasperated by my distress—or, more precisely, by my perception of the moths as a problem to solve. I am the one who deals with practical problems: the shopping list, the sheets that need changing, the moths. But you do not think of these as problems.

I buy two big plastic containers and pack our clothes into them, layered with bags of dried lavender, the scent of which is supposed to repel moths. One box for your clothes and one box for mine. You resist this system, but your clothes are not precious to you. I insist. You make me feel frivolous for loving what I have laboured over, which I resent. I recognise for the first time a fundamental difference between us: our conceptions of the word *frivolous*.

All of this is irrelevant. You are desperately unhappy because we have been stuck inside for most of a year. I am unhappy because I cannot solve this, or anything else, and I am the only one who perceives any problems. More than anything, I long to be offered softness.

⁌

Foolishly, I've been keeping my fabric in a cardboard box. I'd forgotten about it in the panic over our wardrobe, but the moths have been here too. A heavyweight piece of linen is riddled with their lacework of hunger. A scattering of holes freckles the edges of a cotton knit, as if punched by a passing ticket collector.

Somehow, miracle, the moths haven't eaten more than the hem of the fine merino I bought on sale at the start of the summer. I freeze it for a week, then cut it hastily into three turtlenecks.

I don't like sewing knits and have been putting off these turtlenecks, even though I know I will wear them almost every day this coming winter. But I don't want my merino to be eaten to dust before I've even worn it.

I switch my universal needle for a jersey one and turn my machine to the zigzag stitch setting. Each top takes less than an hour. They are the softest clothes I own.

⤳

Just before Christmas, the lockdown ends. A few weeks later, so does our lease. We disagree on whether to move—I think we need to; you can't be bothered—but ultimately we do. I go to the viewings alone and choose a flat some distance from our old one. The new house has no moths, but we bring other problems with us.

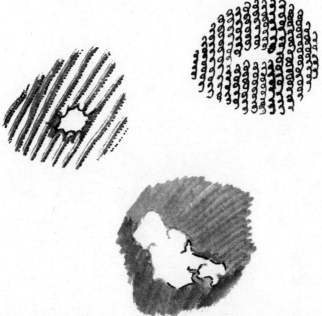

Silver Lining

*Double-faced grey plaid and fawn
wool coating, silver viscose, dark grey
polyester thread, silver polyester thread,
heavyweight fusible interfacing,
30 mm black corozo button //
The Fabric Store Poppy Coat*

THE FIRST CHILL OF AUTUMN IS IN THE AIR WHEN I move in with 婆婆 | Por Por. She urges me to hang my clothes in the wardrobe, but I don't want to take them out of the suitcase. On the first day, when I feel like hiding in a small, dark space for hours, she makes me chicken for dinner and says, with unbearable concern, 麗麗 | *Lai Lai, now you will not get married*, to which I say—absolutely nothing.

I decide to sew something complex and labour-intensive to keep my sadness only a shadow while my hands make something of nothing. Several months ago, I decided I would make a TFS Poppy Coat come winter: an oversized, proper cold-weather coat, with a single button closure and a big soft rounded collar. It's not winter yet but I'm cold all through and half my clothes are still at the old flat, so I start the coat.

Coats are my favourite type of garment because they represent a kind of escapism. Auckland is never really cold enough for a coat, but nonetheless wearing one in grey July makes me think of snow falling on woollen shoulders, as it does in all the cities I'd like to live in. More importantly, wearing a coat means feeling held. A coat is protection against weathers external and internal.

I've never been good at sewing slowly—it's too exciting to go fast—but I don't get a choice here. I print the pattern in Ao at a local copy shop. Then, on Instagram, I look at Poppy Coats made by sewists around the world. Poppies cut from old woollen blankets, shearling with checked lining, lilac cashmere. I read all the captions and take notes on recurring advice: size down two to three sizes; practise the pockets; use a point turner and press every seam. I lay out my fabric, a heavy brushed grey wool plaid, bought months ago on sale, and steam it with patience. Perhaps, for once, I will do it all as I should.

The Poppy Coat is the most difficult garment I've ever made. It takes me a whole morning to learn to make welt pockets, those funny formal rectangular pockets you get on school blazers or the backs of suit trousers. I smooth my grandma's sputtery iron over many metres of interfacing, a lengthy process with pattern pieces this big. I cut my lining—a liquid, silvery viscose that slithers wildly under the chalk—on the hard white tiles of the bathroom floor, the pattern weighted with library books. By the time I have sewed the shell together and it looks like a coat, with functioning pockets and half the collar, I've been sitting at the machine for seven hours, so long I can barely straighten my neck anymore. The wool is too heavy to press the seams open properly, and the bobbin thread keeps snapping because I'm sewing three thick layers too quickly, and, on second thought, perhaps I've snipped just a millimetre too far into the corner on one of the welt pockets, which means I'll need to patch the back before I put the lining in. But the coat is a coat, made for my body by my hands.

Like gardening, sewing is an investment in the future—in what sort of person your future self will be, and how she will feel about her body, and what she will want to wear. I choose this grey plaid and cut it to my size thinking unashamedly of myself and how I want to feel, which is not how I feel now.

More fundamentally, as writer Sofi Thanhauser puts it, 'Sewing something for yourself implies belief in a future self.' Pressing the lining today means I will stitch it into the outer shell tomorrow. Inserting a pocket now means one day it will hold my hand. I clip into the collar corners; learn and execute the finicky couture of buttonhole stitching by hand;

wrestle determinedly with the petulant lining. Sewing means proving to myself I haven't given up on either work or joy.

My cousin Lisa is also making a coat. We share one sewing relative—her grandmother, my great-grandmother—who died when we were small. But both of us remember her knotted hands, which cooked 炒饭 | chao fan for sixty years, and tended the garden, and made the whole family's winter coats. Lisa is making a Papercut Patterns Nova Coat of two contrasting black and brown tweeds. Her coat is minimalistic, a clean cocoon shape, while mine is sweeping and romantic. She reminds me that another sensibility entirely is possible. We sew our coats together, and on the days we are apart we send each other progress pictures—us in half-coats, in single sleeves, threads bird-nested at hems, everything unfinished and promising. It is just what I want.

Lisa finishes her coat before me and sends me a picture taken in front of her bathroom mirror. She looks fantastic. It remains amazing to me that this silly little hobby of ours could turn out something that looks like an actual coat. When I next see her, she's wearing her coat out in the world, an idea made real. It looks as good as anything you could buy, but she shows me how, at the hem, where the lining meets the shell, there's a slight misalignment: a reminder it was made by inexpert hand. I think this is quite beautiful in her coat, but when I attach the lining of my own coat to the shell and it's similarly crooked, I feel annoyed. I hate this feeling and this month I'm tired of my feelings—and after unpicking the seam twice, I end up letting it be. I move on to the next step, so eventually I can send Lisa a photo taken in front of 婆婆's bathroom mirror.

I don't know what to make of this slip of time. I rise each morning at six; I read before work; I make small, simple meals. The rice cooker lisps beside the stove; the orchids pose stark and flowerless in the living room. The washing machine plays an irresistible electronica version of "Die Forelle" to announce the end of a cycle. I enjoy my enjoyable job, I save money, I have not one single drink, and in many ways, I feel good. On the other hand, I still wake too early every single day, in the middle of a panicked half-dream in which I am looking and looking—inside my suitcase, beneath the bed, in the drawer in the old apartment where I kept old keys and shopping bags—for something I've lost and cannot have back.

The day I finish the coat, I've been living with 婆婆 for a month. She grew up in an era when you sewed not for pleasure but because you couldn't afford to buy clothes, and so she's amused by the coat saga. Every afternoon, she calls one of her many friends for a gossip—about what so-and-so paid for her house, which family member has caught Covid now, and me. She still hasn't realised I can understand almost everything she says in Cantonese. I hear her telling everyone she knows that for some reason I am making a coat, and that she'd like me to stay.

Ease

Black and beige gingham cotton,
black polyester thread, 4 cm elastic //
Anna Allen Pomona Pants

KATE AND CRYSTAL, MY NEW FLATMATES, WANT to go out dancing. I haven't been dancing for years and possibly never in the way they mean. Kate and Crystal are both much cooler than me and I'm waiting for them to notice—but they haven't, not yet. They promise it will be fun to stay up late and meet a bunch of strangers and I mostly believe them. Kate and Crystal want to spend an hour getting ready, painting wings on their eyelids and glitter across their cheekbones, arranging their bodies for maximum enjoyment. Their laughter silvers the whole house. Kate and Crystal want to get tipsy enough that life feels loose and bright. They are younger than I am. They both have whole wardrobes for going out dancing, among which there is not, God forbid, one jumper. In their crocheted bikini tops and patchwork jeans, their rings and fanciful tattoos and monster truck sneakers, they look incredibly alive. They offer to lend me something but their clothes feel like costume. Over the past two years I've sewed a wardrobe of day clothes for a journalist. But we're going out tonight and I can't dance in a midi dress. I need something I can do shots in, something I feel attractive in, something I can make quickly.

Sifting through my patterns, I feel the old thrill of resourcefulness. I choose the elastic-waisted Pomona Pants, a pattern I've had cut out for months, and a big cotton check I got at a sewists' swap. Two pattern pieces. No side seams. Faux flat-felled seams. Big cup of tea. I skip the pocket: tonight I won't carry a thing. It takes just ten minutes to cut out and an hour to sew. I know my shape well by now, so I make my pattern adjustments swiftly, unconsciously—scooping the front crotch, shortening the rise. I insert the elastic with more ease than usual so I can breathe deeply and eat whatever the fuck I want—we are friends these days, my body and me. It's sheer, rushing pleasure to go this fast. I want to run and run, until I overtake myself and all the old hurts. I want a whole new identity I can make in one day. It doesn't feel impossible.

When I twirl in the finished pants, Kate and Crystal scream. They hatch a plan for us to hit on strangers tonight, something I've never done. No part of me wants to tempt the possibility of a connection, which ends, which hurts—but perhaps Kate and Crystal know something I've forgotten. They are the brightest people in my life right now because they met me only a month ago. They don't think I'm lost. They pump up their music with the windows wide open and order a pizza and pour me another and tell me the pants look *so fucking good*. They lend me eyeshadow. The air fizzes in the Uber. I wear my new pants with a crop top and sneakers, and we dance and dance and dance.

Cut One Pair

Forest green linen, forest green polyester thread // McCall's #7969

IT'S OCTOBER, UNSEASONABLY WARM, EVERY-thing tumultuous. After six months, our lease is ending and we're all reluctantly going our separate ways. My room is half packed when Lisa comes around, everywhere shameful cauls of dust. But Lisa loves a bit of disorder. She's come to take us to the opshop.

Lisa is the sort of person who says things like *Maybe you need to have more casual sex* and *How's the old anxiety today?* She owns a clock shaped like a piece of naan and a lot of semi-ironic hats. As a sewist, she's brave: brave enough to wing a coat lining or make a whole outfit the morning before the event she needs it for. She texted to organise this outing twenty minutes ago.

We make these impromptu trips out for sewing supplies at least once a month—partly because one of us always genuinely needs something to finish a project, and partly so we can enable each other to pick up something unnecessary. Lisa calls the outings *rampages*. We comb the opshops of West Auckland for vintage patterns and wildly underpriced lengths of old silk. Sometimes we go to an actual fabric store—usually Drapers on Khyber Pass, where Lisa has won over every single member of staff—and dream among the rolls. We're shopping for ideas. Always we spend more than we should.

Today, among the dilapidated board games and lone knitting needles, Lisa finds a cream-coloured quilt to turn into a jacket and a vintage bedsheet she'll eventually wear to someone's wedding. I find a heavy white tablecloth embroidered with sprays of flowers, which I immediately see as a boxy top.

After a quick lunch of two bao each, wolfed down leaning against the wall of our go-to spot, we head back to Lisa's and I retrieve my sewing machine from the boot of her car. We put the fabrics we've just bought into the washing machine and get on with other projects. Lisa is chaotic and I'm pedantic, but we're both the sort of sewist who has at least three garments on the go at once.

Today Lisa is sewing an oversized jumpsuit in a heavy, claret linen—a mash-up of the Helen's Closet Gilbert Top, a short-sleeved shirt with a collar, and the balloon-legged Style Arc Bob Pants. Unusually for her, she's bothered to make a calico toile—a practice run for rehearsing the inseam length and deciding where to end the button placket. Now she traces the pattern onto her precious linen and cuts it out while I distract her hyperactive griffon, 弟弟 | Dae Dae. I'm sewing a swoony, billow-sleeved dress in forest green linen: the McCall's #7969 pattern with an added skirt tier. Lisa would never make this hyper-feminine dress and I would never make her jumpsuit. But sitting in the same space, the differently pitched chugging of our machines tangling together with Lisa's hip-hop and the quick-fire conversation we shout at each other over the noise—*Do you reckon he's worth a second date? Do you have any chocolate?*—I think of the word *companionable*.

Occasionally we'll ask each other a sewing question. Lisa wants to know whether the waist should be higher. I'm trying to remember that technique I saw somewhere for flat-felling inseam pockets. At these points, whoever is being asked the question will set down their work and come over to help. When necessary, one of us restrains the dog, who is sneezing from all the thread. We take turns standing in front of the mirror, trying on half-garments. Because we're together, we're pernickety: we hold each other to a higher standard. Do I really need pockets? *Yes*, says

Lisa, *on principle*. I add them. Should she bother with French seams, or half-arse it with zigzag stitching? *French seams*, I insist, and she complies.

At some point, the washing machine will finish, its ancient beep floating upstairs, sending 弟弟 absolutely wild. We hang out our spoils to dry, then stop for snacks—no small occasion, because Lisa works for a snack foods company and will lay out a whole platter of experimental biscuits she's working on as well as chips in discontinued flavours. We ingest copious amounts of sugar and sodium. We make teas and forget about them. We gossip.

We sew a bit more as the afternoon gets on, although we rarely finish a project when we're together. We'll both finish later that evening, alone in our separate rooms, and swap photos over Instagram. Sometimes I think I'm only sewing for the satisfaction of Lisa's all-caps reactions.

Before I head home, we retrieve our dry fabrics from the line. Even here, in the moment of exhaustion, they look like potential: another afternoon like this one, please.

Undoing

*Assorted textiles
and notions //
Assorted patterns*

THE YEAR IS SOFTENING INTO YELLOW SUMMER when I catch Covid and get sicker than I can ever remember being. I'm too weak to get out of bed to turn off the light so it stays on all the time, the shadows playing malevolently across the wall. I watch *Kiki's Delivery Service* over and over and dream that I too live in an indeterminate Central European town, wearing a black smock dress and little red shoes.

After two weeks I emerge back into my life, which suddenly feels impossible. My lungs can't handle the long runs I rely on to maintain my sanity. More than once, in the middle of an interview I lose my train of thought and have to ask the question again—and when I try to marshal my stories into sentences, they splinter like the edges of fine silk.

I crave the sense of achievement that comes from making something new. But when I go to make the summer shorts I've been planning for ages, I sew two whole left legs, only realising my error when I go to join the crotch seam. I fuck up the topstitching on the pocket, twice. I break needles and waste thread. My hands won't obey me. Again and again, I take out my unpicker, this ugly shard of plastic hidden behind every success, and snap the threads. I start over.

In my bleaker moments, I count my failures. There have been so many since I started sewing. There was the dress with the too-high armpits, which made me feel like a sausage in casing. All those misaligned waistbands and puckered sleeve caps. The nap of the velvet facing the wrong way. My troubles with the tension on my shirred dress, the thread that kept snapping, the heartbreak. Worst of all is when I make a fully functional garment that just doesn't suit me—a True Bias Shelby Dress in too-virginal white linen, or a Vikisews Oona Dress, squeezing me in every wrong place. I give both dresses away, but my smaller failures—things fixable with the most boring kind of labour; mistakes embarrassing and tedious—sit mostly unresolved in a tote bag under my bed.

For a whole month, I stop sewing. I'm so tired. I don't want to be productive anymore; I want to rest. The whole world wants to rest: everybody is deleting their Twitter accounts, moving to the countryside, quitting their jobs. One day, almost on a whim, I quit my job. The constant deadline, present through all my hours, has become unbearable. I apply for a Master's in creative writing, confusing everybody, including myself. I won't hear about the programme for another month. I consider picking blueberries for the summer.

During my last month at the magazine, I turn to mending. A terrible dress becomes a less terrible skirt. I snip out the deodorant-stained armholes on two tank tops and rebind them lower; I let out the back darts on an overfitted pair of trousers. Every garment is one I made when I knew less: I find I can forgive myself now for my earlier errors. No mending job is exciting, exactly, but I like the metamorphosis of a new garment from within each mistake.

After Covid, sewing is noticeably more embodied than before. I seem to live, quivering, in the delicate tendons of my ankles and the back of my neck. The slightest tilt of my wrist changes how fast the machine feeds the fabric its stitches. My foot knows exactly the pressure to apply to the pedal. Sometimes, in impatience, I push harder than I should, causing the machine to gobble a length of linen with a harsh sound. After an hour, my back aches and my eyes are tired of focusing. I am sensitive to pain these days and have to lie down. Hours pass in this way.

Just before Christmas, I hear that I've got into the Master's programme and will be moving to Wellington in two months. I read the email in my last week at work, sitting at my desk with the latest recipe proofs, floating above my body. They will pay me a stipend to live on so I'm allowed, for a summer, to rest. I walk to Grey Lynn Park and lie under the oak trees, not minding that I'm still ill.

Gently, eventually, I finish the mending pile. I make the right leg of my shorts. I begin to run long distances again, slow and even beside the blue water. I grow steady, awaiting the next change.

Bound

*Scarlet linen,
scarlet polyester thread //
Liam Patterns Robin Dress*

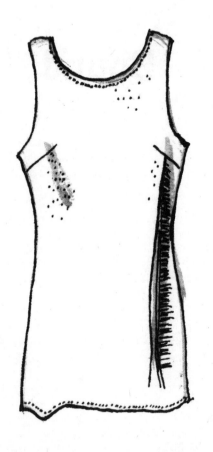

THE DAY BEFORE THE LUNAR NEW YEAR, AND TWO weeks before I leave Auckland, 婆婆 | Por Por rings me in a panic. She hasn't been able to find mandarins at the supermarket underneath her apartment block, and without them the New Year is unthinkable. Will I go to buy six? I go to the Dahua on Dominion Road, which is absolutely heaving. Amid the lanterns decorated with cavorting rabbits and the man chopping up 烧乳猪 | roast suckling pig and the shining bins of plums and apples, there's a whole display of out-of-season citrus: yellow-green local mandarins, orange imported ones, mandarins with the leaves still attached. I buy the six most beautiful specimens I can find.

This year our family is having a low-key celebration. 婆婆 is ninety now, too old to prepare all the traditional dishes, so instead she orders dim sum from her favourite restaurant, the one where the manager always comes over, beaming, to say *Hello*, 好好好.

We will eat at the Formica table in her apartment under the faded photographs that have been in my life forever: my young and radiant grandparents in front of their new house; my mother and uncles in graduation regalia; the kindergarten portraits of each grandchild.

I've eaten dinner with 婆婆 under those photographs every Friday for the last year. We don't talk much. I feel guilty every week that my Cantonese isn't better. She asks about my new flatmates; if work is busy. I ask her about when she was young, and her recipe for 云吞 | wontons. She tells me that when she first came to Auckland, aged nineteen, she took the tram to English classes after work. She loved the classes, not because she liked learning English, but because the tram was a thrill, and the classes were the only time she saw other Chinese girls her age. She tells me about running the fruit shop on Karangahape Road in the 1960s, how some customers were kind and others were unkind, how early she had to get up. As a child, she rarely left her village. She remembers the arrival of the Japanese and drinking a cabbage soup she hated every winter. She cried all night after her father pulled her out of school because he did not believe girls needed educating. Her 云吞 are made with pork, prawns, corn starch, sugar, ginger, garlic, shiitake mushrooms, spring onions, and soy sauce measured by eye. She makes me repeat back the ingredients in Cantonese—猪肉, 虾, 玉米淀粉, 糖, 姜, 蒜, 冬菇, 葱, 豉油—and praises me when I'm done. When I tell her I'm moving to Wellington, the first thing she says, before *You leave your job?* or *Where?* is *I miss you.*

The day before the New Year, I'm struck with the need to make this year special. I want to wear something vital, photographable; something in that lucky Chinese red, the colour of 利是 | red packets and lifeblood. I don't own any red clothing, but I have a metre of scarlet linen, bought on sale without specific plans, eye-ticklingly bright in my stash.

I wonder about making my own cheongsam, which seems appropriate for this holiday. But traditional Chinese garments have always felt like dress-up to me; I'm not quite comfortable in a cheongsam. Is this because I'm only half-Chinese? Why do I think of the word *only*? I feel more Chinese than usual during the New Year, but still not quite enough to belong without consciously deciding I do. Still, I could never pass for white, and this year, for the first time, I'm glad.

I run the idea of making a cheongsam past Lisa, who says something unexpected: *You're not half of anything*. Still, she suggests, the eleventh hour might not be the right time to start a garment. I should definitely toile. She suggests making a Liam Patterns Robin Dress instead, which she's recently had great success with—a slinky little mini cut on the bias. She drops round the paper pattern for me so I don't even have to print it.

A metre is not really enough fabric for this dress, but I make it work by cutting, sacrilegiously, slightly off the true bias. In my haste, I disregard all the best practice advice about using pattern weights and cutting on a properly flat surface. But the dress is a good choice: a simple sheath of colour, a body made bright. I use slightly bumpy bias binding for the neckline and armholes rather than fussing around with facings, and the back darts turn out kind of pointy, like I have four back nipples. But the whole dress, mistakes included, takes just one evening to make, my triumphant FINISHED message to Lisa sent at 9.07pm. I send her a picture wearing the dress with my thready socks and no bra. *Gorgeous*, she promises.

When I get to 婆婆's apartment with my bag of mandarins the next morning, her eyes widen as she opens the door. 你好靓! | *Nei hou leng!* she says, before anything else. She washes the mandarins carefully and stacks them into a little pyramid to tempt prosperity. As we are setting the table, she grips my arm tightly without saying anything. She does not understand why I quit my job or left a five-year relationship. Such prospects do not come around twice, in her experience. But she's decided to accept me without understanding: my Caucasian eyes, my penchant for drinking cold water straight from the tap, my decision to go back to university at the age of twenty-seven. *You look beautiful*, she is saying, and it is the highest compliment she could give.

Use

Recycled black nylon, multi-coloured viscose, charcoal polyester thread, 20 mm brass snaps // Hacked Paola Workwear Jacket

I DRIVE THE EIGHT HOURS FROM AUCKLAND TO Wellington with my whole life in my car. The sewing machine is rattling around in the back seat and all my fabric is squashed into one big plastic container, layers of calamine pink linen and black cotton corduroy and cream denim scraps laid down like sediment. Even with the limited space, I can't bring myself to throw away the scraps of earlier projects.

I move to a suburb called Kilbirnie. My flat is on the side of a hill and you can see the sea looking out of the window in both directions, a small, grounding fact. There's almost a month to go before my degree starts and I don't really know anyone in this city, so I take myself around as a tourist. I'm properly lonely for the first time in a while and have to keep telling myself, *One day at a time.* I make a pair of dark jeans with red topstitching and half a classic white shirt, but I don't really feel like it.

The weather is different here. Throughout February, supposedly the middle of summer, it rains on and off in icy sweeps. The wind could carry you down the street. I swim in the sea most days, an old habit, but the white-whipped waves dare me otherwise. Waiting at the bus stop under a flimsy umbrella, I realise I need a raincoat. Something sturdy and dark. Long enough to keep my legs dry. *Dress for the conditions*, I tell myself briskly, as if I'm on a hike, one that's going to end with a spectacular view.

Despite an afternoon spent researching patterns, I can't find any raincoat designs I like. Have raincoats always been so blatantly practical? I just want something that looks like an ordinary coat, with an added hood. No drawstring at the waist. No faux fur trim. I know I prefer the aesthetic of a coat with closures up the front—a long, snaking zip or bright snaps or buttons—rather than a pull-on anorak, and it would be helpful if it were a free pattern. Then it comes to me: I'll hack the Paola Workwear Jacket, a tried-and-true classic in my wardrobe. I'll just need to lengthen it, add a back vent and hood, and draft an extra placket flap to keep the wet from getting in through the buttonholes. It's exactly the sort of project I need to keep me busy and out of the wind.

While it rains, I toile my raincoat in calico, cutting it out of the toile I made for my Poppy Coat last year. I'm a student now and money is tight again. I'd like to make the final coat out of dry oilskin, an environmentally friendly waterproof fabric, but it's more than $50 a metre. I settle on a recycled nylon instead, black and practical and the best I can afford. I decide it will be prettier than the fabric suggests—sometimes you have to decide these things.

Meanwhile, everything changes. I learn this lesson over and over and it never becomes less surprising. Classes start and twice a week I sit in a room overlooking the sea with ten other writers, discussing the things we've written and read, trying to figure out whether and why they move us. I feel for the first time in years that I'm bringing my whole brain and heart to each day's work. I walk everywhere, make a friend who braves the freezing sea with me. Twice a week, I work as a dishwasher in a bakery. After hours of scrubbing sheet pans in scalding water, my fingertips grow raw and every textile becomes extraordinary to my hands—from the nubby grit of the calico toile to the faint cross-hatch on the nylon. I eat too many pastries. Life softens.

For two weeks in March, I seem to split my time exactly between sewing and writing. In the mornings

I turn paragraphs. In the afternoons I set seams. I'm trying to write a big, difficult essay about family: I advance and unpick, advance and unpick, never quite saying what I mean. It's different work from sewing a raincoat. It seems to bring me into a different knowledge of myself, to offer some kind of progress, although there are no illustrated instructions for writing an essay and at the end you have nothing to hold. But my raincoat will keep out the rain. I change the patch pockets for ones with flaps, so the water will run right off. I draft a deep hood so I can wear my headphones and a beanie underneath on the walk to uni. Over one painful afternoon I draft a back vent, so the raincoat can be as long as

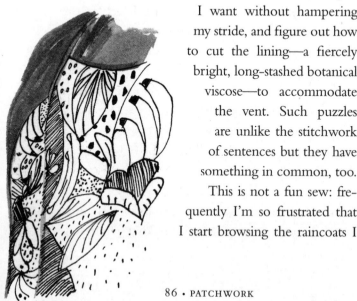

I want without hampering my stride, and figure out how to cut the lining—a fiercely bright, long-stashed botanical viscose—to accommodate the vent. Such puzzles are unlike the stitchwork of sentences but they have something in common, too. This is not a fun sew: frequently I'm so frustrated that I start browsing the raincoats I could buy online. Perhaps I would cave, if I could afford it. It rains on many days before the coat is finished.

The day I finish the raincoat, setting in the snaps first thing in the morning, my essay isn't finished but I think I know what to try next. I walk to uni with half a draft in hand, raincoat folded in my bag, just in case. Both have their uses. My heart is open.

Cut One Self

*Crimson silk satin,
crimson polyester thread //
Liam Patterns Carol Dress*

SINCE STARTING TO SEW, I CATCH MYSELF NOTICing other people's clothes more. The ethereal white wrap dress over black underwear. The fitted denim flight suit with brick red topstitching and Docs. There's a girl wearing a velvet baby doll dress with a sheer blazer and big owly glasses on the bus. She gets off outside the Botanic Gardens. Where is she going?

They say things, these clothes. They say, *Fuck me* or *Don't look at me* or *I'm creative and I want you to know it*.

Clothes as armour, clothes as invitation.

Making clothes takes things a step further. Sewing is a kind of productive daydreaming: *Maybe I could feel this way, if I made this garment for my body. Maybe I could be this kind of person.*

The clothes available to buy are limited, but you can make anything you can think of. Sewing is imagining, not just assembling, a self into being. Who knew you had so much self to express?

You always knew.

Q: *What is your favourite garment you've made?*

A: *A Paradise Patterns Hallon dress in terracotta linen. It's got a high neck and a low back and I wear it with a little crop top underneath. It's comfortable, it's easy, it's casual, it's a little bit sexy. It just makes me feel really good. Sometimes I wear it because I already feel good and it's an expression of that. Sometimes I put it on to make myself feel good.*

My favourite thing to sew is a bias-cut slip dress.

A dark colour, French seams, a lustrous textile.

Ideally, it's fluent and shining even on the hanger and makes me feel beautiful when I wear it.

I know wanting to be beautiful in the sense of desirable is fraught, an abdication of the self because it locates value in the judgements of others. But I mean beautiful in a wider sense. Wearing a bias-cut slip dress makes me feel touchable, yes, but it's also about how the fabric feels against my skin—its cling and surf; its location of my waist and hips.

It makes me conscious of my body as sensation rather than visual object. My body feels like it's mine. And it makes me feel elegant, more able to regard the world with grace, like I'm going to an event that demands a poise I love to give.

The dress gives me back to myself.

Q: *What is your favourite garment you've made?*

A: *I love the tiered skirt I made last year because it was so much better than I'd expected and it felt imbued with my mother's affection for me, because she gave me the fabric and helped me use it. I think particularly because she wouldn't give any of my other siblings fabric, although she might send them things as gifts, it felt like my mother knew me as someone who wants to live in the things I make.*

I love making a bias-cut slip dress, although I once didn't think I was a bias-cut slip person.

I didn't think I had the body for a slip. But who decides which bodies can wear slips?

The sewist decides what they will wear. They reassert it in the execution of every detail.

I spend a whole day's wages on a luscious deep red satin and choose a pattern—the Liam Patterns Carol Dress—with a sweeping neckline.

I'm thinking of clothes that perform selves I'd like to be: Keira Knightley's green dress in *Atonement*, the sleeveless floral cheongsam Maggie Cheung wears in *In the Mood for Love*, glittering Adele at the 2012 Grammys. My dress will look nothing like Keira Knightley's green dress, but I hope it creates the same feeling. A pulsing, living colour, desire made textile.

Slip is the right word, somehow. Liquid, unsteady, given to movement.

I will wear it with my hair out.

⤳

Q: *What is your favourite garment you've made?*

A: *I love the various linen tops I made in rusty oranges and mustard yellows and swampy greens because they taught me about the palette I feel great in, rather than having to wear colours that are having a moment in fashion or sticking with grey-blues because they were 'safe'.*

⁓

The instructions for this slip dress do little hand-holding and the pattern has no lengthen/shorten line, so I have to wing it. But somehow I breeze through.

I surprise myself by seeming to have crossed some kind of threshold, beyond which I understand how to make a slip dress. It's become intuitive to under-stitch the facing so the neckline won't roll outwards, to hold bias-cut fabric steady so it won't pucker under its own weight, to French seam anything involving silk.

These are skills it takes nothing but practice to master, like all of sewing.

I have practised and practised.

⁓

Q: *What is your favourite garment you've made?*

A: *I love my simple black merino turtleneck for dispersing the long-held belief I can't wear high-neck tops (whatever can't wear means).*

It takes me just four hours to finish my slip dress, from cutting out to final press. It will need hemming in the morning—all bias-cut garments need to hang overnight. But I put it on in the mirror and feel how it feels: smooth and cool and shapely.

I wear it to lie on my bed and read, a girl in a beautiful dress.

Common Thread

*Floral viscose, black cotton poplin, black
polyester thread, midweight fusible
interfacing, 10 mm self-covered buttons //
Porcupine Patterns Qipao*

I LISTEN TO AN EPISODE OF THE *ASIAN SEWIST Collective* podcast in which they discuss the history of the 旗袍 | cheongsam (qipao in Mandarin), a traditional Chinese dress. I learn that the cheongsam likely evolved from a loose, ankle-length robe worn by Manchu women during the Qing dynasty. In 1912, a group of female students in Shanghai began wearing modified cheongsams, which resembled long men's robes, to protest for gender equality. By the 1920s, the garment was trendy; by the 1950s, it was a standard day dress style both in China and among the Chinese diaspora, worn by everyone from ordinary citizens to movie stars. The garment had adopted the Western-influenced shape usually associated with it today: figure-hugging, midi length with side slits, featuring a mandarin collar, and fastened across the chest and down the side with traditional 盘扣 | pankou (knot buttons), zips, or snaps. Now, among Chinese communities, the cheongsam is usually reserved for wear on special occasions.

I've never been particularly attracted to the high-necked, fitted shape of the cheongsam, which is only ever shown on thin bodies. I also associate the garment with a kind of female Asian servitude—cheongsam-style dresses are often worn by Chinese hotel staff or flight attendants—that feels one wobbly step away from fetishisation. As co-host Nicole Angeline says in the *Asian Sewist Collective* podcast episode, 'The qipao seems to serve as shorthand for sexy and exotic.' But I long to make a garment that connects me to my heritage.

Online, I see many BIPOC sewists making beautiful versions of cultural garments or incorporating culturally significant sewing techniques or fabrics. At times like these the Instagram sewing community, always a source of style inspiration, seems particularly precious for showing me other sewists feeling out their cultural identities. A few years ago, I interviewed a Korean-American sewist named Netty (@small.sews) who had made her own modernised 한복 | hanbok in the softest shades of beige and light green. When I first saw it on my Instagram feed, I gasped out loud. 'Growing up as an Asian-American, I don't think I fully understood the importance of my cultural heritage until I was older,' she told me. 'A hanbok back then to me was just a pretty dress, but as an adult, I understand how important maintaining my cultural identity is.'

I crave this same feeling of connection in making a cheongsam but I want to wear it, too. I would never wear a traditional cheongsam. I would feel like I was 'cosplaying a Chinese person', as my flatmate Rose says—and I don't want to invite any racist comments. I wonder if there's a way to make something more subtle.

Instagram tag-stalking reveals that plenty of sewists have taken the cheongsam and run with it. Blogger The Pankou experiments with streamlined cheongsams in striking colours, often swapping the pencil skirt for something swishier. Writer and sewist Nina Mingya Powles (@sewingwriter) has made a short, modernised cheongsam in blue and white cotton that retains the mandarin collar and bias binding finish, but features an A-line skirt that finishes above the knee. I find cheongsams made of black scuba knit (@sophie.sews), cheongsams with bishop sleeves and tie closures (@jesssewukno), cheongsam bodices hacked onto tiered skirts and styled with clogs (@dearsamfu). I'm interested in all these tweaks—the way they have a different charge for a cultural garment, and the way they remind me that a cheongsam is still fundamentally a piece of clothing, tweakable in the way all garments are.

For my own cheongsam, I use the free Porcupine Patterns Qipao pattern as a starting point. It's not very accessible—offered only up to a 104 cm hip, and you have to add the seam allowance yourself—but it's the only cheongsam pattern I can find that's produced by an Asian pattern-maker, Singaporean Yi Farn, which feels important.

I heavily hack the pattern. I lose the mandarin collar in favour of a mock collar, cutting the neckline of the bodice high and drafting a facing. There will be no visible bias binding or piping, no 盘扣—instead, I decide on rouleau buttons, a notion I've wanted to try for months. I straighten out the skirt shape, cut it to knee length, and omit the side slit. I hate installing invisible zips so I decide the buttons will start with the diagonal chest closure, then continue down the side of the bodice and skirt. My fabric, a swooshy dark floral viscose, is busy enough to soften most of the design lines.

Somehow this becomes the most finicky, annoying garment I've ever made—a reminder, after the success of my slip dress, that I'm no master sewist. Each step stymies, as if the fabric doesn't want to be a cheongsam or can sense my apprehension.

When I first attach the sleeves and try on the bodice, I can't lift my arms above my head. *The* HUBRIS, I think grumpily to myself, *of not making a toile.* I realise I forgot to add the seam allowance to the sleeves so I have to recut them—only I don't have enough leftover fabric for both sleeves and have to scrappily piece the underside of one. Next it turns out I haven't cut the mock neck large enough and I feel choked. I insert two triangles of extra fabric at the side seams to widen the top of the neck hole, but then making a facing to accommodate the triangles is impossible. I opt for bias binding instead, but accidentally bind the whole neckline closed before remembering I need to leave the front open so the bodice has two crossover pieces.

At least there are the button loops, which involve nothing more than sewing one long, thin tube of fabric, turning it right way out, and snipping it into 2.5 cm lengths—but my loop-turner is missing. I substitute a knitting needle, then a chopstick, but succeed only in poking several holes in my line of stitches. *Fuck sewing*, I think. One lone, pathetic tear tickles the back of each eye.

It takes me a whole week to return to my cheongsam. Once I've unpicked the neck hole, rebound it in two sections, and pinned the crossover bodice and skirt together, I try it on. It fits and I don't look like an air hostess but I don't look comfortable, either. It looks—the words I'm thinking are *too Chinese*. I prickle with shame. Somehow I look like I'm performing myself, like I don't quite have a right to this outfit. It makes me terribly sad that I could feel more comfortable in a bias-cut slip dress than even a modernised cheongsam.

I take it off and eat a Kit Kat in my underwear. Then I locate my loop-turner in the bottom of my scraps box, turn my long tube, cut it into loops, and stitch them into the placket I've drafted. I attach thirty self-covered buttons; I roll the baby hem. I am neat and grouchy. It is, at least, beautifully finished. I decide to call it a wearable toile.

I wear the cheongsam to uni the following week under my raincoat, with tights and a bright beanie. Doing up the buttons is a pedantic pleasure, a reminder, with each slipping into place, of my perseverance. Ella tells me she likes my dress. Then Lou does. Catching sight of my reflection in a window, I wonder if I've overthought things. It looks like I'm wearing a high-necked tea dress. It's pretty. I don't know if it's something I would wear if it weren't a cheongsam, but I'm trying on a part of myself and it doesn't feel terrible.

The next week, trying to finish a poem, I find myself sketching a tank top—one with a diagonal cross-chest closure, fastened with ties. I remember a metre of black cotton poplin at the bottom of my stash, crisp and sober. Using just the bodice section of the Porcupine Patterns Qipao, sides straightened and two inches added to the length, it takes me only an hour to sew up.

I put it on in the mirror, paired with dark jeans and boots: a cheongsam of sorts; a cheongsam for an uncertain girl. I know, looking at my reflection, that I'm not done figuring anything out. I will make many more cheongsams, some leaning traditional, some getting as far away as possible. I want to wear this garment. I choose this self. Perhaps the choosing matters more than the being sure.

Care
Instructions

*Cobalt linen, cobalt
polyester thread, midweight
interfacing, scarlet cotton
embroidery thread //
Traced off ready-to-wear*

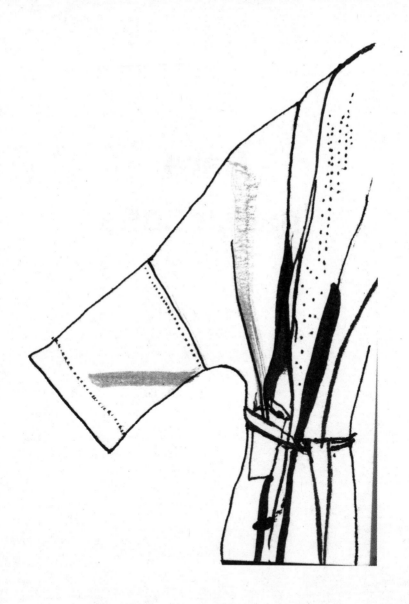

IT'S HER BIRTHDAY IN THREE WEEKS AND I DON'T know what to get her. We are recent friends, friends of only a year's standing, but I think she will be in my life forever. I would like to give her something that wishes the length of that forever.

I decide to make her a dressing gown, like a full-length, portable hug. I choose a cobalt blue linen, her favourite colour, so intense it hurts to look at, and spend more than I should—but I've decided money is for spending on loved ones. When the fabric arrives a week later, I wash it and hang it to dry on the line, dimpled with sun. It's almost too beautiful to cut.

I cut more carefully than usual, bothering to iron first, and lay the fabric out on the flat tiles of the bathroom rather than just the carpet. I trace the pattern off my own shop-bought dressing gown, then add a back pleat so it will float behind her, and shorten the sleeves a little so they won't trail when she's making her coffee. I cut tiny rectangles of fabric to make belt loops and a loop for hanging. I cut vast pockets, for holding snacks and notebooks and her phone when she needs to flip the pancakes. I remember all the little details I would skim past if I were making this for myself. I stitch care into every seam.

On our free afternoons together as time-rich students, we walked everywhere with our eyes wide open. We gathered flowers to press; drank the coastline. We sat with little cups of coffee and licked cinnamon and sugar off our fingers. Sometimes we went to one of the luxury shops in town, scented with leather and perfume. We had no money for elegant things—linen sheet sets, handmade bowls—but we looked until we were full.

When we met, I thought she was unknowable: shy, a little hesitant. But I read her work and she read mine and we became close. I learned that she was commuting each week from Palmerston North, a town two hours from Wellington. My flatmate was going away, so I offered the spare bed. She accepted.

Each Tuesday she arrived with her bag—toothbrush, change of clothes, notebook, swimsuit—and we traded the week's news and drank tea. We learned poems by heart. We walked shrieking into the sea in the middle of winter. We split the cost of dinner.

We roasted chickpeas under olive oil until rich and jammy; we soy-cured eggs and split them over steaming bowls of noodles and greens. Together we rolled the dough for cardamom buns, inhaling the spice until heady. She never arrived without bringing something she had grown: tiny purple potatoes, cordial made from the elderflowers in her garden, a bucket of lemons. Before this year, she had planned to be a market gardener. Near the university she stopped along the path to say, *So beautiful, the kōwhai; look how much wild fennel!* Her eyes saw the ruru in the trees, no matter the depth of darkness.

We spent our whole lives in different cities, and one year in the same. Now, our degrees finished, she's heading north while I stay here.

When I ring, I hear the sunnier half of her news. She's been making chilli oil, building a new bookshelf, sewing—by hand—a seersucker dress. Where she is, in rural Maratoto, seven hours' drive away, she is isolated. Her partner, a conservation ranger, is often away and she hasn't found a job yet, isn't sure of the shape of her year. I don't like to think of her unsteady, surrounded by rain and bush. When I was unsteady this year, she took my hand; sat at the end of my bed and offered her quietness. *My love, you are brave*, she said. Held out my dressing gown.

A dressing gown will hardly fix everything, but I make it with maximum fierceness. I French seam everything, so all the raw edges are held. I backstitch firmly, so nothing will unravel. What was loose and vague becomes reliable; fixed. When I'm nearly finished, I embroider one looping, cursive initial, *L*, in red on the inside of the collar, to be held against her skin. *Dear heart*, I am saying, *you are brave*.

Patchwork

*Assorted textiles, assorted
polyester thread, cotton
wadding, cream mercerised
cotton topstitching thread //
Self-drafted*

FOR THE BEST PART OF THREE YEARS, I'VE BEEN saving Instagram photos of other people's patchwork. A purple and green quilt with ribbon lettering spelling out an immortal Frank Zappa lyric (@hemelbreker). An extra-squishy linen quilt, natural-dyed using indigo, madder, and sumac (@stone__soup). An enormous checkerboard quilt framed by flying geese blocks, made to mark a cotton wedding anniversary (@laura.wolfgang). Korean pojagi-inspired patchwork hangings of many small squares in soft colours (@deborahmanson). The untitled patchwork pieces of Louise Bourgeois. Even more than clothes, quilts seem to edge into the realm of art.

Quilts are closely tied to community—both because they preserve community stories and because they can be worked on by many hands at once. I'm fascinated to learn that communities across the world create various forms of patchwork, passing a set of techniques and aesthetic tendencies down the generations: from intricate Miao wedding quilts to densely stitched Welsh quilts to the irregular, colourful blocks of Gee's Bend quilts.

The very existence of certain quilts records and insists on certain communities, including communities that might otherwise be marginalised. As such, quilting is inherently political. The AIDS Memorial Quilt, for instance, started in 1985, commemorates the lives of people who have died of AIDS-related causes. Each of the 50,000 panels has been contributed by someone in grief and love. And I'm stopped cold by a series of photos of quilts made by the indigenous Sioux and Lakota people of North and South Dakota on Jess Bailey's Instagram page (@publiclibraryquilts). Bailey, an art historian and author of the excellent *Many Hands Make a Quilt: Short Histories of Radical Quilting*, writes that quilting, seen as a 'civilised', 'European feminine' craft, was forced on many indigenous people as the US government tried to eradicate their culture. Indigenous people, who had their own traditions of patchworking animal skins, used popular quilt storytelling techniques to record their experiences of settler colonialism in the blocks of lone star, log cabin, and crazy quilts. 'I think quilts are good at absorbing trauma,' writes Bailey. 'The quilt is a record of violence, a tangible material memory.' Of course, quilts are also a literal source of warmth and physical comfort—a metaphor made cloth.

Traditionally, across many different cultures, quilts are gifted at moments of obvious, public change, such as weddings or the birth of a child. But when Bailey asked the Instagram community what else quilts could mark, she crowdsourced many other answers. An abortion. A miscarriage. A hysterectomy. A first period. Grieving somebody you didn't get to say goodbye to. A platonic relationship anniversary. A birthday in a hard year. Coming out. Moving away. Release from prison. Finishing a PhD. Quitting a PhD. Unionising. Recovering a mother tongue. Starting therapy. The end of a relationship—whether abusive or loving.

Quilt as record, quilt as story. Quilt as making meaning of suffering or uncertainty. Quilt as love, quiet but certain. I want to make a quilt that honours these ideas, one that marks all the changes since Covid. I'm not sure yet who I will gift it to, but the making will be just for me.

I will make my quilt mostly from scraps, which I've been accumulating since my first Demeter Dress. I settle on a design of moons. There will be eight rows of eight moons each, the moons in each row progressively either waxing or waning. I want the multivalence of moons: moons for the passing of time, moons for the female body, moons for longing. The moon as cipher for that city in an e. e. cummings poem where 'everyone's / in love and flowers pick themselves'. Moons for tides, in every sense.

The quilt starts with maths, never my strong suit. I figure out the seam allowances, then cut out sixty-four blocks in greens and pinks and blues and purples. I pair the coloured squares and cut them into moons at various stages of the lunar cycle: each convex crescent has a corresponding concave crescent to spoon in a contrasting fabric. No two blocks are the same. I want the randomness of this: vanilla next to citrus, pale pink beside forest green. The quilt remembers all my earlier projects. It remembers now, too: pairing these old fabrics on the living room floor; listening to The Beths;

my flatmate Rose, also a sewist, making a colour-blocked sweatshirt beside me.

Eventually I'll join all my blocks together, maybe add a frame in a contrasting colour. I'll plump up my wadding, choose a backing fabric, and stitch everything together by hand with a meandering running stitch. I'll enclose the edges with bias binding, slip-stitched invisibly to the main. But tonight I'm still making the quilt blocks one by one, a breath further each day.

Edge

*Khaki cotton twill,
grey polyester thread,
22 mm coconut button,
20 cm YKK zip //
Mood Fabrics Adair
Cargo Pants*

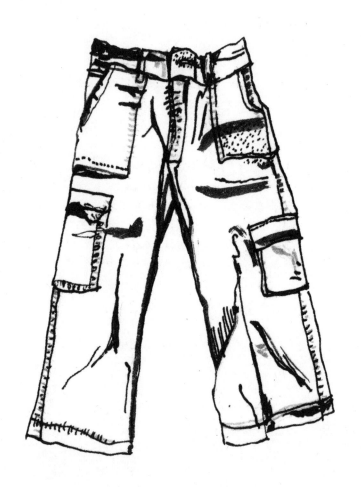

AFTER A YEAR IN WELLINGTON, I FIND MYSELF leaning towards darker clothes. I want to dress for this city, which feels like home now—and the city is full of stylish people wearing black. In their midst, I consider wearing dark nail polish and cutting my hair short. I want to mark myself as an inhabitant of this place.

My friends joke that this could be my edgy summer. Rose gives me a black mesh top she never wears. I cut an old slip dress daringly short and dig out my Doc Martens. The shops are full of edgy clothes this year: oblong sunglasses, oversized T-shirts, parachute pants that swish when you walk. The silhouettes are wide and androgynous. I'm resistant to the idea of following any trend, which feels particularly wasteful when you're sewing your own clothes, but I'm not convinced this will be fleeting. I suspect I'll always want a part of my wardrobe to feel moody and genderless and invulnerable.

I don't have trousers that fit me anymore so I decide to make some cargo pants, something loose-fitting and practical. My fabric—I couldn't resist—is a durable, camo-print cotton twill, only semi-ironic. I print the Adair Cargo Pants, a free pattern from Mood Fabrics. Its six pockets—four with flaps—promise these will be pants as much about function as aesthetic. I like the idea of making a garment that lets my body feel less scrutinised—a garment that appears confident and a little sulky. Some days, you want to be thought of as beautiful; others, you want armour. *Cargo pants in camo print?* says Rose, cutting pockets for a jumpsuit out of fluorescent green corduroy. After a whole year sewing side by side, I'm still tickled by the differences in our taste. *You're crazy*, she says. But I'm thinking about how good it feels to wear something 'out of character'. How freeing it is to discover there's really no such thing as out of character, because you can change that character at will.

I sit at the dining table with my machine, my pile of pattern pieces on the next chair. This is my permanent spot now, this left-most chair at the edge of the table, scissors and pin box to my right, ironing board against the wall. I start by assembling the pockets and their flaps: twenty-two lines of topstitching, grey on green. The instructions for this pattern are sketchy at best, but I take it slow and trust my instincts. I assemble the fly—always the hardest part of a pair of pants—using the YouTube video I watch every time.

When I'm tired, I'll stop for the day. These pants will be the work of three or four sittings; I'm in no rush. Outside, December unfurls bright and blue in a mass of sea swims and coastal runs. I have no idea what I'll do for work next year, where I'll live. The future seems to demand a bravery I'm sometimes not sure I have. In the meantime, I'm here with my machine, cloth in hand. I set the stitch, like so many before me. I try to trust.

Notes

THE INFORMATION ON TEXTILE PRODUCTION AND wastage in "Moral Fibre" comes from two sources: a report by the Ellen MacArthur Foundation, *A New Textiles Economy: Redesigning Fashion's Future* (2017), which can be found at ellenmacarthurfoundation.org/a-new-textiles-economy; and an article by the Global Living Wage Coalition, 'Industry: Garment/Textile', Global Living Wage Coalition (accessed May 1, 2023), which can be found at globallivingwage.org/industries/garment-textile/.

The Sofi Thanhauser quote in "Silver Lining" comes from her article "Sewing and making clothes can inspire, heal or bind us to the past" in *The Guardian* (February 26, 2022, https://www.theguardian.com/lifeandstyle/2022/feb/26/sewing

-and-making-clothes-can-inspire-heal-or-bind-us-to-the-past).

The italicised sections in "Cut One Self" come from interviews with my friends and fellow sewists Gabrielle Amodeo, Shanti Mathias, and Lisa Young.

Earlier versions of "Second Skin" and "Silver Lining" were published by SWAMP in 2023.

Acknowledgements

A HUGE THANK YOU TO MY FELLOW SEWISTS—IN person and online—for teaching me how to French seam a split hem/install an invisible zip/stop for the day, cheering when I ace a make, and providing endless inspiration. Special thanks to Lisa Young for all the madcap hooning around Tāmaki, limited edition biscuits, and sage advice. I'm ridiculously glad to be related to you.

To my MA cohort—Lou Annabell, Ella Borrie, Jess Clifford, Caitlin Daugherty-Kelly, Maddie Fenn, Gráinne Patterson, Poppy Saker-Norrish, Hattie Salmon, and Joseph Trinidad—and tremendous supervisor, Chris Price: thank you for your thoughtful feedback on some of these essays right at the end of the process. I still can't believe I got to spend a year with all of you, and your writing.

Thank you to the wonderful teams at The Emma Press and Tin House for taking a chance on this book, and for all your support throughout the process! Special thanks to James Trevelyan, Georgia Wall, Peri Cimen, Masie Cochran, Nanci McCloskey, Beth Steidle, Jacqui Reiko Teruya, Becky Kraemer, and Isabel Lemus Kristensen for all your care and enthusiasm, to Emma Dai'an Wright for all the above and the gorgeous illustrations, and to Emma and Dassi Zeidel for invaluable copyediting on both sides of the Atlantic.

Thank you to the flatmates I lived with while I thought about, wrote, and (seemingly endlessly) rewrote this book: Kate Bodger, Crystal Amor-Ponter, Arianne Zilberberg, Carole Roussel, Jason Parker, Rose Lu, and Paddy Wilson. It seems incredible we were ever strangers. Thank you for keeping me sane and putting up with all the thread.

To my friends: you're all bloody wonderful. Among a million, million things, thank you for making me laugh so much, buying me sugary snacks when I'm sad, daring me to stay up later, and believing I could write a book. I wonder how I got so lucky every single day.

Special thanks to those friends who spent hours of their lives going over an earlier version of *Patchwork* with a fine-tooth comb: the book is so much better for you. Gabrielle Amodeo, everything you make is beautiful. Shanti Mathias, you have the sharpest eye and more ideas than anyone I know. Weiling Zhong, thank you for so many years of friendship, and all your help with the Cantonese characters. And Sophie van Waardenberg—how could I ever say it all? I love you terribly. Thank you for knowing what I mean better than I do myself.

Finally, thank you to my family. For putting up with me; for everything.

CELESTE FONTEIN

Maddie Ballard is a writer and editor of mixed Chinese heritage. Born in Syracuse, New York, she grew up in Aotearoa New Zealand and currently lives in Melbourne, Australia.